THE SPIES, CODES AND SECRET ORGANIZATIONS DURING THE AMERICAN REVOLUTION

History Stories for Children
Children's History Books

Speedy Publishing LLC

40 E. Main St. #1156

Newark, DE 19711

www.speedypublishing.com

Copyright 2017

In this book, we're going to talk about spies and codes during the American Revolution. So, let's get right to it!

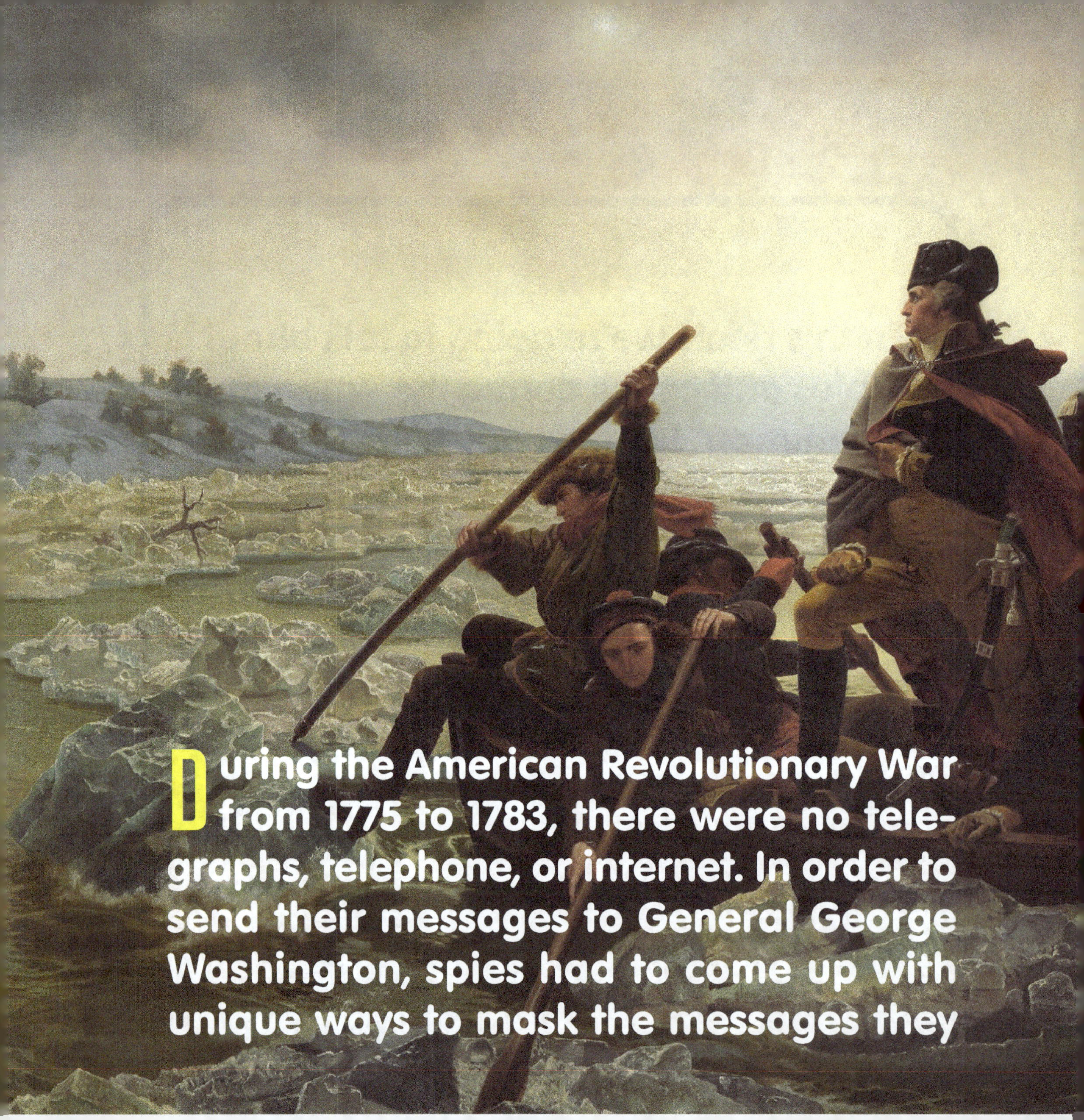

During the American Revolutionary War from 1775 to 1783, there were no telegraphs, telephone, or internet. In order to send their messages to General George Washington, spies had to come up with unique ways to mask the messages they

were sending in written letters on paper.
Letters could always be intercepted and,
if they were, the enemy would know and
possibly be able to change strategies in
time.

A SECRET CODE IN THE WALL

The methods that the spies used to hide their messages were ink that was invisible as well as secret codes. They also used mask letters, which required a special template placed on top of them so that you could figure out the hidden message within the letter. These three ways of keeping messages hidden from the enemy worked and Washington developed a successful spy ring during the war.

INVISIBLE INK

Sir James Jay was a doctor and politician. He was also the brother of John Jay, one of the Founding Fathers of the United States. He created an ink that you could see on paper as you were writing but that when dry would be invisible.

YOUNG SPIES IN WASHINGTON CITY

A special chemical had to be used on the ink to make it possible to read again. At the beginning, James was sending secret messages to his brother to warn him of the actions the British were going to take. Eventually, spies working for Washington used the ink.

SECRET CODES

★ ★ ★

Washington's spy ring used a secret code to relay their messages. The code consisted of seven hundred and sixty-three numbers to represent certain words, places, and names. Messages were sent back and forth with these secret codes.

SECRET CODES

I-SPY SECRET CODE BOOK COVER

In order to decode the messages, spies needed a codebook that translated all the numbers into their correct words. The code and codebook were developed by Major Benjamin Tallmadge who was the spymaster of Washington's ring of spies based in New York. Although, this type of code can be broken by a process called "frequency analysis" there is no record of the British deciphering Tallmadge's code.

MASK LETTERS

Mask letters were the most complicated of the types of messages to send. The letter would have to be written just as a piece of normal correspondence. However, the receiver would have had a mask or template that went over the letter with a hole in it. For example, one type of shape was an hourglass opening. Once this opening went over the letter, the words that were in that shape had a hidden message that was hiding in plain sight within the original letter.

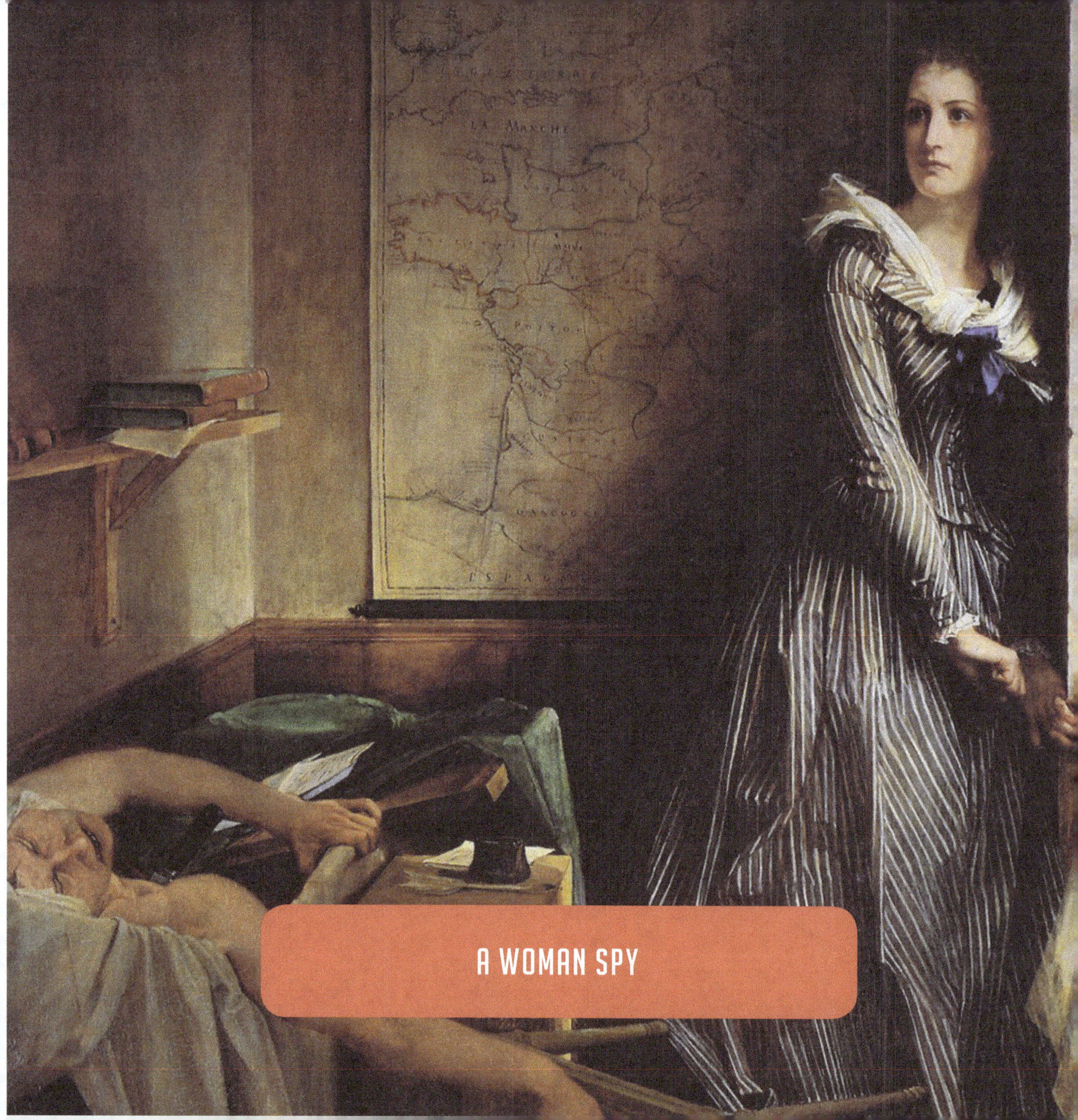

A WOMAN SPY

DISGUISES AND COVERS

On both sides, spies needed to use disguises to get information from the enemy. They sometimes used fake names and posed as local people in order to infiltrate enemy groups. Women were spies as well. No one suspected them so they were able to over-hear information and relay that information to the spy ring.

They even had a designated number in the Culper Code Book, which was 355, the word "lady." The identity of one of the woman secret agents was never verified. She was only identified as 355. Being a spy was very dangerous because the penalty for spies that were captured was death.

Word / Place (cut off)	No.		
…arth	718	a	e
…, Lord	719	b	f
…ain do.	720	c	g
…John	721	d	h
…Saml.	722	e	i
…Junr.	723	f	la
…oe	724	g	b
…mister	725	h	c
…ivington	726	i	d
Places		k	o
…York	727	l	m
…Island	728	m	n
…het	729	n	p
…bridge	730	o	q
…en	731	p	r
…Island	732	q	s
	733	r	t
…Island	734	s	w
…necticut	735	t	w
…Jersey	736	w	x
…ylvania	737	x	…
…ryland	738		
…ginia	739		

N.B. the use of this Alphabet is where you wish to express some words not mentioned in the numerical Diction[ary] for instance the word *heart*. would [be] expressed thus *biels*. look the letter[s] of the real word in the first column of the Alphabet and then opposite to them, let those letters in the second columns repre[sent] them; in this case always observe to draw a line under the word, as *sine*. stands for *buter*.

Numbers are represented by their opposite letters which must have a double line under them as *siks* is 2456. & *ngw* is 790. — — — In the numerical Dictionary it is sufficient to express a part of a sentence only in figures, to make the rest perfectly unintelligable. all words cannot be mentioned th[erefore]… meaning must… to be found, & the[y]… not proper to be wrote, then the[y]…

STATUE OF CAPTAIN NATHAN HALE

CULPER SPY RING

In 1776, the war was not proceeding as planned. Washington and his troops had been pushed out of New York City. He needed intelligence about future British plans and war strategies. He sent Nathan Hale on a mission to get this intelligence, but Hale was discovered by the British and hung for treason.

With the help of Major Benjamin Tallmadge, whose spy ring name was John Bolton, Washington launched the Culper Spy Ring. The name of the ring was invented by Washington who had adapted it from Culpeper County in the state of Virginia. The intelligence that this group was able to communicate throughout the war was a critical factor in the ultimate victory of Washington and his troops.

BENJAMIN TALLMADGE

DANIEL BISSELL

MEMBERS OF THE CULPER SPY RING

DANIEL BISSELL

Bissell joined the British Army and worked for them for over a year as he gathered intelligence. He had pretended to be a deserter from the Continental Army.

BENJAMIN TALLMADGE (ALIAS JOHN BOLTON)

In addition to being the leader of the ring, Tallmadge was a successful military officer. He led a raid on Long Island that ended in the Battle of Fort St. George. After the war was over, he was a representative in the new US government.

BENJAMIN TALLMADGE

HESSIAN CAPTIVES

ABRAHAM WOODHULL (ALIAS SAMUEL CULPER SENIOR)

Woodhull traveled from Setauket to the city of Manhattan under the guise of visiting his sister. The British began to suspect him and went to his home to arrest him but he wasn't there. He brought Robert Townsend into the ring.

ROBERT TOWNSEND (ALIAS SAMUEL CULPER JUNIOR)

Now that Woodhull had almost been discovered he had to find ways to keep his movements more secret. He enlisted Robert Townsend who began sending information to Woodhull's farm via courier. A historical researcher discovered Townshend's true identity in 1929 after doing handwriting research on correspondence.

EXECUTION BY FIRING SQUAD

SURRENDER OF LORD CORNWALLIS

SALLY TOWNSHEND

Sally Townshend was Robert Townshend's sister. Her father Samuel Townsend was forced to quarter British officers in his home called Raynham Hall. Sally fell in love with one of the British officers by the name of John Graves Simcoe.

The officers were using her home to pass secret messages. One of the messages implicated Benedict Arnold, who was commander of West Point. Arnold would betray his country by giving information about West Point to the British. When Sally found this message she was torn but she knew she must do the right thing. She gave the information to her father who passed it to Tallmadge. Supposedly, her ghost still haunts Raynham Hall.

BATTLE OF LONG ISLAND

ANNA STRONG

ANNA STRONG

Anna Strong was also involved in getting information to Woodhull. She was his friend and neighbor and used a unique method to communicate. A black petticoat hung up on her clothesline meant that a boatman was ready to leave and he was carrying secret information. The number of handkerchiefs on the line indicated the cove where he was waiting.

CALEB BREWSTER

Caleb was the boatman who watched for Anna Strong's signals. His job was to travel across the Long Island Sound to relay secret messages back and forth. Woodhull would meet him at the designated cove to pick up the messages. Brewster and Tallmadge were both childhood friends of Woodhull.

BATTLE OF GUILIFORD COURTHOUSE

THE BATTLE OF FONTENOY

MARY AND AMOS UNDERHILL

Mary Underhill was Woodhull's sister. She and her husband Amos ran a boarding house and were also involved with collecting intelligence for the ring.

AGENT 355

To this day, no one knows who Agent 355 was. Perhaps someday a historical researcher will be able to unmask her.

Austin Roe is known as the "Paul Revere of Long Island." His job for the ring was to ride the 55 miles between Setauket and New York City to carry secret messages. To avoid being found out, he pretended to be a merchant conducting business. In 2015, a letter was found that also identified Austin's two brothers, Nathaniel and Phillip as participants in the ring.

AUSTIN ROE

BATTLE OF BUNKER HILL

HERCULES MULLIGAN

A clothing store owner in New York, Mulligan would pay attention to his British customers, many of whom were British officers. He then passed on any vital information to Washington.

OTHER IMPORTANT REVOLUTIONARY SPIES

NATHAN HALE

While Nathan Hale was getting information for Washington, he was caught by the British and hung for treason. He is known for the famous last line, "I only regret that I have but one life to lose for my country."

NATHAN HALE SIGNATURE

MOLLY PITCHER

LYDIA DARRAGH

While British officers were meeting in her home, Lydia paid attention to their war strategies. She promptly turned the information over to the Patriots.

FASCINATING FACTS ABOUT THE CULPER SPY RING

★ ★ ★

The Culper Spy Ring operated from late 1778 to 1783, the time when the British departed New York City.

The group was located on Long Island, New York in the city of Setaukat. Their messages were relayed mostly in New York and in Connecticut. Their mission was to send Washington important information regarding the British troop movements in the area.

BATTLE OF LEXINGTON

BENEDICT ARNOLD

The ring discovered that General Benedict Arnold was going to go over to the British side. They also discovered that the British were planning to attack troops from France who had just arrived as reinforcements. Another important piece of intelligence was that the British had plans to create counterfeit Continental money.

Washington never forgot what happened to the great patriot Nathan Hale. He didn't want to see any other spies lose their lives and insisted that the utmost secrecy apply to all communications to minimize risk. In fact, the group was so secret that even Washington didn't know all the group's members!

HANGING OF NATHAN HALE

GEORGE WASHINGTON

George Washington left the day-to-day operations of the ring to Tallmadge but he also managed the operation of the ring on occasion.

For the most part, the ring was made up of Tallmadge's trusted childhood friends and colleagues from Long Island.

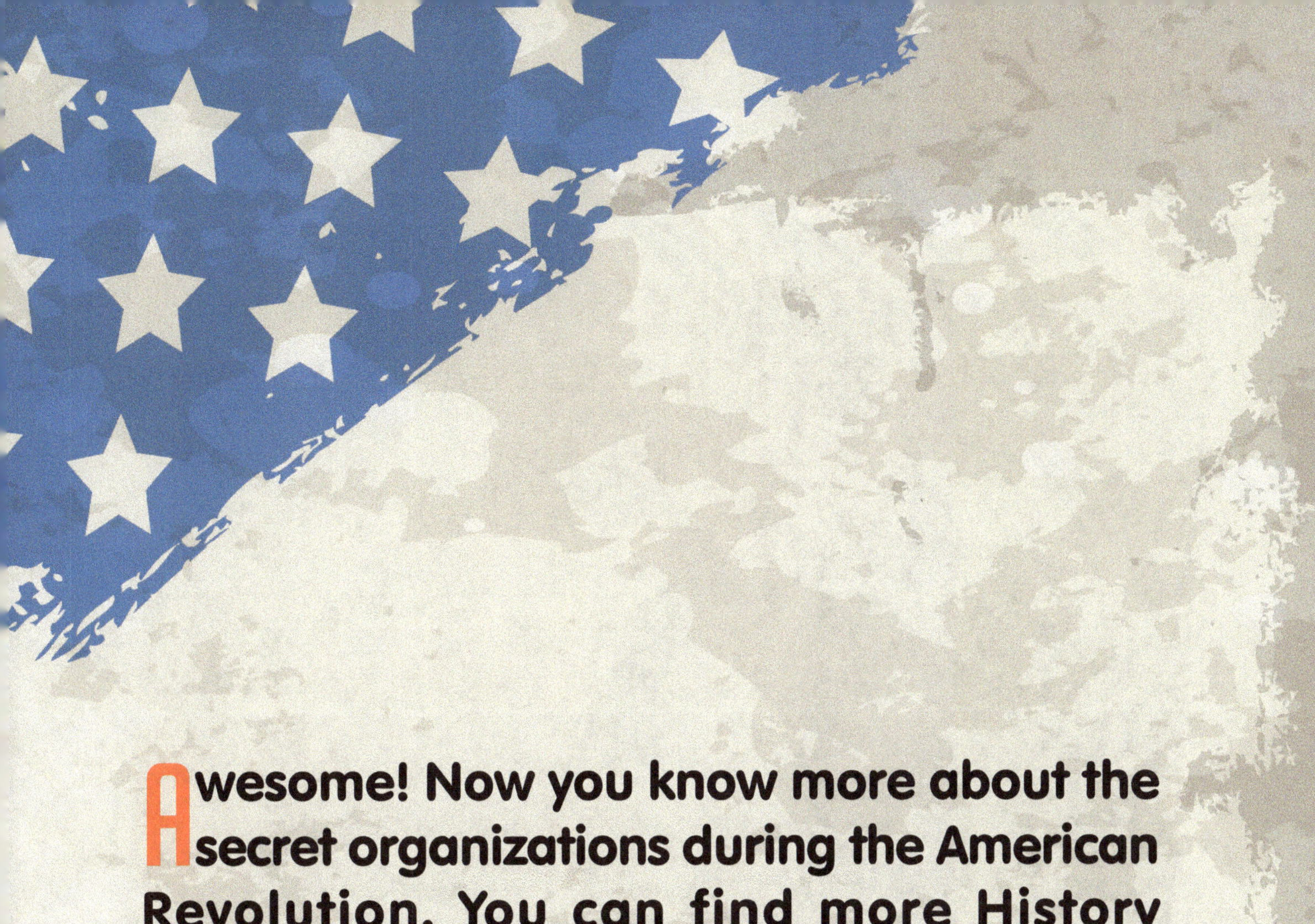

Awesome! Now you know more about the secret organizations during the American Revolution. You can find more History books from **Baby Professor** by searching the website of your favorite book retailer.

Visit
BABY PROFESSOR
EDUCATION KIDS
www.BabyProfessorBooks.com
to download Free Baby Professor eBooks and view
our catalog of new and exciting Children's Books

9 798869 430724